FOOD BRANDS WE LOVE

FRITO LAY

By Kaitlyn Duling

Kaleidoscope
Minneapolis, MN

The Quest for Discovery Never Ends

This edition is co-published by agreement between Kaleidoscope and World Book, Inc.

Kaleidoscope Publishing, Inc.
6012 Blue Circle Drive
Minnetonka, MN 55343 U.S.A.

World Book, Inc.
180 North LaSalle St., Suite 900
Chicago IL 60601 U.S.A.

Kaleidoscope ISBNs
978-1-64519-209-1 (library bound)
978-1-64519-277-0 (ebook)

World Book ISBN
978-0-7166-4187-2 (library bound)

Library of Congress Control Number
2020936264

Developed and produced by Focus Strategic Communications Inc.

Printed in the United States of America.

Bigfoot lurks within one of the images in this book. It's up to you to find him!

TABLE OF CONTENTS

Chapter 1
Snack Time

The cafeteria was loud. Mac was nervous. It was his first day at the new school. He didn't have any friends yet. He shuffled inside the cafeteria and looked for an open seat. There was one in the very back, at the corner of a long table. Mac sat down and unzipped his lunch bag. Turkey sandwich. An apple. Carrots. Chips. Fritos were his favorite. Mac's dad knew that the corn chips would make Mac's day a little better. Mac happily crunched on his chips. Yum.

It is always a nice surprise to find corn chips in your lunch bag.

Frito corn chips are made by frying corn dough.

All over the cafeteria, kids opened up bags of chips. Many of them came from the same company: Frito-Lay. The chips made at Frito-Lay factories are crunchy, salty, and tasty. Some are made with corn. Others are cheesy. Frito-Lay even makes pretzels and popcorn. Two of the most popular snacks are Lay's and Cheetos. In the US, Lay's varieties make up over one-third of all potato chips sold. That's a lot of chips.

FUN FACT

Each year, Frito-Lay uses enough potatoes to reach the moon and back.

As Mac munched on his chips, his mind wandered. He remembered eating Doritos at a sleepover with friends from his old school. The cheese dust got all over his hands. He thought about the bags of SunChips his mom packed for picnics. He thought about sweet Frito-Lay snacks, too. He loved to eat Cracker Jack at baseball games. Frito-Lay started out with corn chips. But the company grew to include 29 different **brands**.

Nacho chips have a distinctive triangle shape.

FUN FACT
Each eight-ounce bag of Lay's potato chips contains four to five potatoes.

Mac's bag of chips was empty. He wiped the salt off his fingers. It was time to tackle the sandwich and apple. Suddenly, a girl sat down across the table. She unzipped her lunch bag and took out…Fritos. "These are my favorite," she said. "My name is Julia. Want a chip?" Mac smiled. Maybe the new school wouldn't be so bad after all.

A bag of Fritos corn chips weighs 4.3 ounces (120 gm).

FRITO-LAY BRANDS

Below are just some of the Frito-Lay brands.

Doritos

Lay's

Cheetos

Fritos

SunChips

Cracker Jack

Tostitos

Funyuns

Grandma's

Rold Gold

Ruffles

Smartfood

Chapter 2

History of Frito-Lay

The history of Frito-Lay starts in the 1930s. Back then, a man named Charles Elmer Doolin made and sold candy. He lived in San Antonio, Texas. San Antonio is in southern Texas, near Mexico. Doolin liked selling sweets. But he was on the search for a salty snack. In 1932, he visited a gas station, where he tried fried corn chips. They were a popular beach treat in Mexico. Doolin loved the chips so much, he bought the recipe. He made the chips in his mother's kitchen. He sold those first Fritos out of his car, a Model T Ford.

FAMILY RECIPES

Early on, Doolin made recipe pamphlets to advertise his chips. Members of the Doolin family helped create the recipes. Each recipe included Fritos. Today, some of them are still popular. Frito Pie Casserole combines chili, cheese, and chips. Fritos Chocolate Crunchies are salty and sweet.

The Model T Ford was the first popular, affordable automobile.

The Frito Company corn chip factory in Texas in the 1930s.

Fritos was taking off. People loved the corn chips. However, potato chips were popular. Herman W. Lay started his own snack food delivery company in 1932. It was based in Nashville, Tennessee. Lay could see that potato chips were a hit. So, he bought recipes and started making chips. He named his business H.W. Lay & Company. It grew fast. Soon, it was one of the biggest snack food producers in the Southeast US.

Both companies were growing. Both were successful. To achieve even greater things, they decided to work together. In 1961, they **merged**. They formed Frito-Lay, Inc.

FUN FACT

The Frito-Lay brand is valued at $14.7 billion.

Then, in 1965, Frito-Lay, Inc. merged with Pepsi-Cola. Pepsi-Cola made soda pop, which paired perfectly with salty chips. The new company was called PepsiCo. Today, PepsiCo sells many different types of food and drinks. Frito-Lay is an important part of PepsiCo. It produces about half of PepsiCo's annual operating profit. That's a lot of chips—and money.

Pepsi-Cola is a perfect match with Lay's snacks.

FRITO-LAY

TIMELINE

1932
C.E. Doolin has his first taste of "fritas," Mexican corn chips. H.W. Lay starts his snack food delivery company.

1948
Cheetos are introduced.

1961
Fritos and Lay's merge to become Frito-Lay, Inc.

1932 1944 1948 1959 1961

1944
Lay's potato chips are first marketed.

1959
C.E. Doolin dies.

1961
Frito-Lay acquires Rold Gold Pretzels.

1965 1966 1981 1991 1996 1997

1965
Frito-Lay, Inc. merges with Pepsi-Cola to become PepsiCo.

1966
Doritos tortilla chips are introduced.

1981
Tostitos tortilla chips are introduced.

1991
SunChips are introduced.

1996
Frito-Lay's main competitor, Eagle Snacks, shuts down.

1997
Baked Lay's are introduced and immediately become successful. Frito-Lay acquires Cracker Jack.

Chapter 3

Snacks Around the World

Potato chips are known as crisps in Britain. Lay's are called Walkers.

Lucy lives in London, England. On Saturdays, she spends time with her grandmother. They go to a little café in the park. Lucy always orders the same thing—Walkers potato crisps. The snack is salty and

The city of London is situated on the River Thames.

FUN FACT
Lay's potato chips have just three **ingredients**: Potatoes, oil, and salt.

crunchy. The chips taste just like Lay's. In fact, they *are* Lay's. Frito-Lay makes and sells chips all around the world. Sometimes they are called Lay's. Other times, they have different names.

In Australia, Smith's potato snack were called crisps until 2003 when they became chips.

José Luis lives in Mexico. After soccer practice, his stomach grumbles. So José Luis stops by the corner store to pick up a snack. He usually buys a bag of Sabritas. They are salty and crunchy. They come in many flavors. Sabritas are also owned by Lay's.

The bag looks just like the one in the US. It just has a different name. The same is true in Australia. There, a bag of Lay's chips is called Smith's.

José Luis knows that Frito-Lay doesn't just have different names for its chips. It also makes unusual flavors. In Mexico, he buys salt-and-lime-flavored Fritos. Someday, he'd like to travel to South Africa. That's where he could find tomato-flavored Fritos. In Canada, he could try ketchup or salt-and-vinegar-flavored Lay's.

There are many different flavors of Lay's chips around the world.

Lay's sold blueberry flavored chips in China for a short time.

Doritos tortilla chips come in a wide range of flavors.

How many flavors are there? There are over 160 flavors of Lay's. More than 100 Doritos flavors have been created. And Cheetos come in at least 50 flavors. It might take José Luis a few years to try them all. For a short time in 2009, Frito-Lay sold blueberry Lay's in China. José Luis isn't too sure about that flavor.

Cappuccino potato chips? That was one of the flavor ideas in the 2014 contest.

FAN FLAVORS

To come up with new flavor ideas, Frito-Lay turns to its fans. The company has held several "Do Us a Flavor" contests. People can submit ideas for chip flavors. Some get turned into chips. The 2017 winner was "Crispy Taco." The 2015 winner was "Southern Biscuits and Gravy." ...Yum?

Chapter 4

The Future of Frito-Lay

Aaron likes to grocery shop with his parents. They let him choose some of the groceries. He gets a different type of cereal each week. He also chooses a bag of chips. In the snack aisle,

Lay's potato chips come in many flavors such as red pepper (papryka) in Poland.

he sees a huge sea of flavors. Most of them are owned by Frito-Lay. The company started over 88 years ago. They still sell Lay's and Fritos. And they continue to create new products. Frito-Lay wants to keep growing.

Lay's Baked Original Potato Chips have a lot less fat than regular chips.

Aaron's brother, Sam, is on the wrestling team. At the store, he picks out Frito-Lay chips that are a little healthier. Some are baked instead of fried. Others are **organic**. Still others are made with natural ingredients. They have fewer chemicals. These healthier options are very popular in the US.

FUN FACT

It takes 11 million gallons of milk to make one year's supply of Cheetos.

CLASSIC FLAVORS

Frito-Lay has been making flavored chips for decades. BBQ flavor was the first flavored Lay's chip. It was added in 1965, followed by sour cream & onion. Today's favorites include dill pickle and ketchup flavors.

Each year, Americans eat over a billion pounds of potato chips, or nearly 7 pounds per person.

Kylie loves chips and snacks. She especially enjoys trying new shapes. She always brings fun Frito-Lay chips in her lunchbox. The Doritos' 3-D chips were puffy triangles. The Cheetos' X's and O's were shaped like letters. In 2012, Kylie tried something totally new. It was the Doritos Locos Taco.

In 2012, Frito-Lay and Taco Bell launched Doritos Locos Tacos.

Frito-Lay partnered with Taco Bell to create a taco shell that tastes just like Doritos chips. It was an instant hit. Kylie loved it.

In recent years, Frito-Lay has branched out. Aaron's family likes to buy Stacy's Pita Chips. They are thick and crunchy. Aaron's brother eats Matador Jerky, a meat snack. And Kylie loves El Isleño, a brand of **plantain** chips. The company may have begun with corn and potatoes. But it has grown into much more.

Each year, Frito-Lay sells more than $500 million in corn chips.

BEYOND THE BOOK

After reading the book, it's time to think about what you learned. Try the following exercises to jumpstart your ideas.

THINK

THAT'S NEWS TO ME. Frito-Lay is always introducing new products, flavors, and ideas. Consider how you learn about new foods and brands. What information can be found in news articles? What about news programs on TV? Where can you go to find news you can trust?

CREATE

PRIMARY SOURCES. Primary sources provide firsthand accounts of an event. Interviews, videos, and photographs are all examples of primary sources. Create a list of the kinds of primary sources you might be able to find about Frito-Lay.

SHARE

WHAT'S YOUR OPINION? The text states that Frito-Lay is an important part of PepsiCo. Do you agree with that statement? Provide evidence from the text to support your opinion. Share your position and evidence with a friend. Does your friend find the argument convincing?

GROW

DRAWING CONNECTIONS. Create a diagram that shows and explains connections between Lay's, Fritos, and PepsiCo throughout the years. How does learning about the brands' histories help you better understand Frito-Lay?

RESEARCH NINJA

Visit www.ninjaresearcher.com/2091 to learn how to take your research skills and book report writing to the next level!

RESEARCH

DIGITAL LITERACY TOOLS

SEARCH LIKE A PRO

Learn how to use search engines to find useful websites.

FACT OR FAKE?

Discover how you can tell a trusted website from an untrustworthy resource.

TEXT DETECTIVE

Explore how to zero in on the information you need most.

SHOW YOUR WORK

Research responsibly—learn how to cite sources.

WRITE

GET TO THE POINT

Learn how to express your main ideas.

PLAN OF ATTACK

Learn prewriting exercises and create an outline.

DOWNLOADABLE REPORT FORMS

Further Resources

BOOKS

DK. *100 Inventions That Made History*. London, UK: DK, 2014.

Harper, Charise Mericle. *Lights, Camera, Cook*! Boston, MA: HMH Books, 2018.

Renaud, Anne. *Mr. Crum's Potato Predicament*. Toronto, ON: Kids Can Press, 2017.

Taylor, Gaylia. *George Crum and the Saratoga Chip*. New York: Lee & Low Books, 2011.

WEBSITES

FACTSURFER

Factsurfer.com gives you a safe, fun way to find more information.

1. Go to www.factsurfer.com.
2. Enter "Frito Lay" into the search box and click
3. Select your book cover to see a list of related websites.

Glossary

advertise: Announce or promote a product or idea.

brand: The name of a product made by a company.

ingredients: Elements that are combined to make a food or dish.

merge: Combine or unite things together, as when two companies become one.

organic: Made or grown without the use of chemical fertilizers or pesticides.

plantain: A banana-like fruit that is larger, less sweet, and more starchy.

Index

PHOTO CREDITS

The images in this book are reproduced through the courtesy of: vkbhat/iStockphoto, front cover (Fritos); givaga/Shutterstock Images, front cover (potato chips), p. 1; Keith Homan/Shutterstock Images, front cover (Cheetos, Doritos), pp. 3, 7 (center), 8, 9 (Lay's Classic, Cheetos, Fritos, SunChips, Cracker Jack, Tostitos, Funyuns, Grandma's, Rold Gold, Ruffles), 13 (Lay's Classic), 15 (top), 19 (Lay's Brazilian Picanha, Lay's Ketchup), 20 (Doritos), 24, 31; foxaon1987/Shutterstock Images, p. 1 (background); XinXinSing/Alamy Stock Photo, pp. 4-5 (top); mikeledray/Shutterstock Images, pp. 4-5 (bottom); Solstock/iStockphoto, p. 6; Hong Vo/ Shutterstock Images, p. 7 (top); stormur/Shutterstock Images, p. 7 (bottom); LunaseeStudios/Shutterstock Images, pp. 9 (Doritos), 19 (Lay's Limon); Darryl Brooks/Shutterstock Images, p. 9 (Smartfood); johnbraid/ Shutterstock Images, pp. 10-11; AS Food Studio/Shutterstock Images, p. 11; UTSA Special Collections, p. 12; Billion Photos/Shutterstock Images, p. 13 (Pepsi); Andre Bonn/Shutterstock Images, p. 14 (top left); Jonathan Weiss/Shutterstock Images, p. 14 (top right); Yeti Studio/Shutterstock Images, p. 14 (bottom left); Fotoldee/ Shutterstock Images, p. 14 (bottom right); Gita Kulinitch Studio/Shutterstock Images, p. 15 (bottom); Ingus Kruklitis/Shutterstock Images, pp. 16-17; urbanbuzz/Shutterstock Images, p. 16 (Walkers crisps); AtlasStudio/ Shutterstock Images, p. 17; Air Elegant/Shutterstock Images, p. 18; Prachaya Roekdeethaweesab/Shutterstock Images, p. 19 (Lay's Salt & Vinegar); Alisia Luther/Shutterstock Images, p. 20 (top); Diane Bondareff/Invision for Frito-Lay/AP Images, p. 21; WDnet Creation/Shutterstock Images, pp. 22-23; David Tonelson/Shutterstock Images, p. 25 (top); P Maxwell Photography/Shutterstock Images, p. 25 (bottom); hiroshi teshigawara/ Shutterstock Images, pp. 26-27; rblfmr/Shutterstock Images, p. 26; PhotographybyMK/Shutterstock Images, p. 27 (inset); Arne Beruldsen/Shutterstock Images, p. 27 (bottom).

About the Author

Kaitlyn Duling loves salty snacks. She has written over 100 books for children. She lives in Washington, DC.